Commonwealth Chronicles

Tales of Unity and Diversity

By: Isaac Banahene Amoyaw

Copyright © 2023 *Isaac Banahene Amoyaw*

Table of Contents

Chapter 1

Introduction to the Commonwealth

Welcome to the Commonwealth Chronicles: Tales of Unity and Diversity. In this book, we embark on a journey to explore the rich tapestry of cultures, traditions, and histories that make up the Commonwealth. This subchapter introduces this remarkable association of nations and aims to provide a comprehensive understanding of what the Commonwealth represents.

The Commonwealth, also known as the Commonwealth of Nations, is a voluntary association of 54 diverse and independent countries. It spans every continent and encompasses over 2. 4 billion people, making it one of the world's most extensive and varied international organisations. While sharing historical ties through the British

Empire, the Commonwealth is not a political union but a unique platform for diplomatic, cultural, and economic cooperation.

The roots of the Commonwealth can be traced back to the mid-20th century when former British colonies sought to establish a framework for collaboration and mutual support. Today, the Commonwealth promotes democratic values, human rights, sustainable development, and peace among its member nations. It serves as a forum for countries to engage in dialogue, share best practices, and address global challenges collectively.

One of the key strengths of the Commonwealth is its commitment to diversity and inclusivity. Its member countries span different continents, languages, religions, and levels of development. This diversity presents a treasure trove of experiences, knowledge, and perspectives that can be harnessed for the greater good. The Commonwealth celebrates this diversity and recognises it as a source of strength, unity, and innovation.

Throughout this book, we will delve into the fascinating stories and narratives that encapsulate the essence of the Commonwealth. We will explore the cultural exchanges, economic collaborations, and political dialogues that have shaped its history. From the bustling streets of India to the serene landscapes of New Zealand, from the vibrant markets of Nigeria to the stunning beaches of Barbados, we will traverse the length and breadth of the Commonwealth to uncover its hidden gems and untold tales.

Whether you are a general reader seeking to expand your knowledge or a Commonwealth enthusiast passionate about its intricacies, the Commonwealth Chronicles provides a captivating and enlightening journey into this extraordinary association of nations. Join us as we celebrate unity in diversity and unravel the stories that bind the Commonwealth together.

Chapter 2

Brief History of the Commonwealth

Formation of the Commonwealth

The Commonwealth Chronicles: Tales of Unity and Diversity

In the grand tapestry of history, the formation of the Commonwealth is a testament to the power of unity and the celebration of diversity. This subchapter delves into the origins and development of this unique association, which has woven together nations across the globe in a shared commitment to peace, democracy, and cooperation.

The Commonwealth, formerly the British Commonwealth, traces its roots back to the mid-20th century. As the sun set on the British Empire, the formation of this voluntary association emerged as a visionary response to the changing world order. It sought to foster friendship and understanding among its member nations while preserving their sovereignty.

The Commonwealth encompasses a rich tapestry of nations, cultures, and histories. From the vast landscapes of Canada to the vibrant diversity of India, from the island paradises of the Caribbean to the vast expanses of Australia, each member nation brings its unique heritage and aspirations to this global family.

One of the cornerstones of the Commonwealth is its commitment to democracy and good governance. Member nations adhere to common principles, including respect for human rights, equality, and the rule of law. Through shared valuTheecome, a beacon of hope, promoting democracy through shared values and collective action ideals and fostering inclusive societies.

The Commonwealth's success lies in its ability to bridge divides and promote forums, such as the Commonwealth Heads of Government Meeting (CHOGM), allowing leaders to exchange ideas, discuss common challenges, and forge partnerships. These interactions have been pivotal in resolving conflicts, promoting sustainable development, and addressing global issues, including climate change and gender equality.

Moreover, the Commonwealth has been an advocate for youth empowerment and education. The Commonwealth Youth Programme has enabled young people to develop leadership skills, engage in community projects, and promote social change. By investing in the next generation, the Commonwealth ensures a brighter future driven by the ideals of unity and diversity.

In conclusion, the formation of the Commonwealth represents the triumph of unity over division and the recognition of the strength that lies in diversity. This global association has provided a platform for nations to unite, celebrate their unique identities, and work towards a shared vision of peace and prosperity. As the pages of the Commonwealth Chronicles unfold, the stories of unity and diversity continue to inspire and shape our shared future.

Evolution and Expansion of the Commonwealth

The Commonwealth, a unique association of nations spanning the globe, has a rich and fascinating history that has shaped our world today. In this chapter, we will delve into the evolution and expansion of the Commonwealth, exploring the tales of unity and diversity that have defined this remarkable institution.

The roots of the Commonwealth can be traced back to the British Empire, which was at its peak during the 19th and early 20th centuries. As the empire began to crumble, a new vision emerged – a vision of an international organisation promoting cooperation, peace, and mutual understanding among its member states. This vision became a reality with the establishment the Commonwealth of Nations in 1931.

Initially consisting of just a handful of countries, the Commonwealth has grown steadily. Today, it boasts 54 member states representing diverse cultures and traditions. From the bustling cities of India to the pristine beaches of Jamaica, from the vast landscapes of Canada to the remote islands of the Pacific, the Commonwealth encompasses a genuinely global community.

One of the key factors behind the expansion of the Commonwealth has been the principle of equality among its members. Unlike other international organisations, the Commonwealth does not have a hierarchical structure, with each member state having an equal say in its affairs. This commitment to equality has fostered a sense of unity and camaraderie among member states, allowing them to work together towards common goals.

Over the years, the Commonwealth has played a vital role in promoting democracy, human rights, and sustainable development. Its various initiatives have facilitated cooperation among member states, enabling them to tackle shared challenges such as poverty, climate change, and conflict resolution.

Furthermore, the Commonwealth has been at the forefront of championing youth empowerment and gender equality. It has created platforms for young people to voice their concerns and ideas, recognising the importance of their participation in shaping the future of their countries. Likewise, it has been instrumental in promoting gender equality, advocating for the rights and empowerment of women and girls across member states.

In conclusion, the evolution and expansion of the Commonwealth have been driven by the principles of unity and diversity. This unique institution has brought together nations from all corners of the globe, fostering cooperation, understanding, and shared prosperity. As we navigate the challenges of the 21st century, the Commonwealth plays a crucial role in building a more inclusive and sustainable future for all its member states and the world.

Chapter 3

Commonwealth Values and Principles

Democracy and Human Rights

In governance, democracy is a beacon of hope, embodying the principles of freedom, equality, and justice. It is a system that empowers the people and allows for the expression diverse opinions and ideas. As part of the Commonwealth, a unique and diverse family, the significance of democracy and human rights cannot be overstated.

Democracy, at its core, is a form of government by the people, for the people. It ensures that citizens have the right to participate in decision-making processes that affect their lives. Through free and fair elections, individuals can elect their representatives, holding them accountable for their actions and policies. Democracy fosters an environment where different voices and perspectives can be heard, encouraging vibrant debates and inclusive approaches.

Human rights, however, encompass the fundamental freedoms and entitlements that every individual should possess. These rights are universal, regardless of race, gender, religion, or socio-economic status. They include the right to life, liberty, education, healthcare, etc. The Commonwealth strives to protect and promote these rights, recognising that they are essential for the well-being and dignity of all its members.

The relationship between democracy and human rights is symbiotic. Democracy provides the framework for protecting human rights, ensuring that citizens have the power to shape their societies and safeguard their freedoms. Conversely, respect for human rights is crucial for sustaining a thriving democracy. A community that respects the rights of its citizens is more likely to foster an environment where democratic principles can flourish.

The Commonwealth, with its diverse member nations, is a testament to the power of democracy and human rights. It is a gathering of countries committed to upholding these principles, even as they celebrate their unique cultural identities. By embracing diversity and championing inclusivity, the Commonwealth demonstrates that democracy and human rights are not mere ideals but tangible realities that can transform societies for the better.

However, it is essential to acknowledge that challenges persist. In some Commonwealth countries, citizens face obstacles to exercising their democratic rights, and human rights violations continue. Through SMS and institutions, the Commonwealth works tirelessly to help the Commonwealth address these issues, providing support and guidance to member states in their journey towards strengthening democracy and promoting human rights.

In conclusion, democracy and human rights are the cornerstones of the Commonwealth's ethos. They represent the principles that bind this diverse family together. By upholding these values, the Commonwealth ensures that its member nations can navigate the complexities of unity and diversity, fostering a shared future where all citizens can enjoy the fruits of democracy and the protection of their human rights.

Equality and Diversity

In a world that is richly diverse, embracing the values of equality and diversity is paramount for fostering unity among nations. The Commonwealth, a global association of countries, represents a unique tapestry of cultures, languages, and traditions. Within the pages of "Commonwealth Chronicles: Tales of Unity and Diversity, " we delve into the significance of equality and diversity, celebrating the remarkable experiences and stories that make up this global community.

Equality lies at the heart of a harmonious society, ensuring everyone is equal and fair, regardless of race, gender, ion, or socio-economic background. The Commonwealth, with its shared commitment to human rights, upholds the principles of equality, recognising its citizen's worth and dignity of all the narratives of our diverse contributors; we aim to shed light on the struggles and triumphs that have shaped the Commonwealth, inspiring a deeper understanding and appreciation for the challenges different communities face.

However, true unity cannot be achieved without embracing diversity. Diversity encompasses the unique perspectives, abilities, and talents that each individual brings to the table. The Commonwealth thrives on this diversity, harnessing its collective strength to address global issues, promote sustainable development, and advocate for peace. Through the personal stories and anecdotes woven throughout this subchapter, readers will gain insight into how the Commonwealth fosters innovation, creativity, and cross-cultural understanding.

From the sun-kissed beaches of the Caribbean to the bustling streets of Africa, the Commonwealth is a vibrant mosaic where differences are celebrated, and commonalities are cherished. "Commonwealth Chronicles: Tales of Unity and Diversity" invites readers on a transformative journey, exploring the myriad ways in which equality and diversity have shaped the past, present, and future of this remarkable global community. By embracing the principles of equality and celebrating diversity, the Commonwealth stands as a shining example of how unity can be achieved through acceptance and appreciation.

Whether you are a general audience seeking to broaden your horizons or a member of the Commonwealth intrigued by the stories of your fellow citizens, this subchapter will undoubtedly ignite a sense of pride and curiosity. It is through underwear a more inclusive future for all. Join us as we embed by understanding and embracing our shared humanity and our unique identities on this journey of unity and diversity, where the tapestry of the Commonwealth comes alive through the voices of its people.

Peace and Conflict Resolution

In the ever-evolving, your ever-evolving world, resolution becomes increasingly vital. Peace goes beyond the mere absence of war; it encompasses harmony, understanding, and cooperation among individuals, communities, and nations. The Commonwealth Chronicles: Tales of Unity and Diversity delves into the multifaceted realm of peace, exploring its significance and the strategies employed to achieve it within the context of the diverse Commonwealth nations.

The Commonwealth, a unique association of 54 nations, shares a common bond rooted in history, language, and values. However, the diversity within the Commonwealth also presents challenges in maintaining peace. This subchapter explores the various aspects of peace and conflict resolution, shedding light on these nations' complexities.

One of the primary factors contributing to conflicts within the Commonwealth is the presence of diverse cultures, religions, and ideologies. These differences and diversity can also lead to misunderstandings and tensions. The Chronicles examine the role of dialogue, diplomacy, and mutual respect in bridging these gaps and fostering peaceful coexistence.

Moreover, the subchapter delves into the role of education in promoting peace. Education is a powerful tool that equips individuals with the knowledge and skills to resolve conflicts peacefully. By fostering empathy, critical thinking, and a deep understanding of different perspectives, education becomes the catalyst for building a culture of peace within the Commonwealth and beyond.

Additionally, the subchapter explores the significance of economic development in maintaining peace. Socio-economic disparities and unequal distribution of resources can fuel conflicts. By addressing these issues and promoting inclusive growth, nations within the Commonwealth can mitigate the root causes of conflicts and create a foundation for sustainable peace.

Furthermore, the subchapter sheds light on the role of international cooperation and the Commonwealth in resolving conflicts. Through diplomatic channels, mediation, and peacekeeping missions, the Commonwealth has played a pivotal role in diffusing tensions and promoting peaceful resolutions.

In conclusion, the subchapter "Peace and Conflict Resolution" in the Commonwealth Chronicles: Tales of Unity and Diversity provides comprehensive explorations of aspects of peace within the Commonwealth. The subchapter highlights the challenges these nations face in maintaining peace amidst their diversity and offers insights into the strategies employed to foster harmony, understanding, and cooperation. Whether you are a general reader or a member of the

Commonwealth, this subchapter aims to inspire and empower individuals to contribute to a more peaceful and united world actively.

Chapter 4

Commonwealth Institutions and Organizations

The Commonwealth Secretariat

The Commonwealth Secretariat is the institutional hub of the Commonwealth of Nations, a unique intergovernmental organisation that brings together 54 member countries worldwide. Established in 1965, the Secretariat is pivotal in fostering unity and promoting diversity among these nations. This subchapter delves into the functions, structure, and significance of the Commonwealth Secretariat, shedding light on its invaluable contributions to the member countries and the wider world.

At its core, the Secretariat works towards advancing the shared values and goals of the Commonwealth, including democracy, human rights, sustainable development, and economic growth. It serves as a platform for member countries to collaborate, exchange ideas, and address common challenges. The Secretariat supports member countries through its various programs and initiatives in governance, rule of law, gender equality, youth empowerment, and climate action.

The Secretariat is headed by the Secretary-General, appointed by member countries and acts as the principal representative of the Commonwealth. The Secretary-General, along with a team of dedicated professionals, ensures the smooth functioning of the Secretariat and oversees its diverse range of activities. These activities include organising Commonwealth Heads of Government Meetings (CHOGM), facilitating dialogue between member countries, providing technical assistance, and conducting research and policy analysis.

One of the key strengths of the Commonwealth Secretariat lies in its ability to bring together countries of varying sizes, cultures, and economic backgrounds. It provides a platform for both small and member nations to have their voices heard on the internet internationally; the Secretariat promotes South-South cooperation, encouraging member countries to share their expertise and best practices for all benefits.

The Commonwealth Secretariat's work extends beyond its member countries. It actively engages with international organisations, civil society, and the private sector to forge partnerships and amplify its impact. By leveraging its vast network and resources, the Secretariat contributes to global peacebuilding, conflict resolution, and sustainable development efforts.

In conclusion, the Commonwealth Secretariat is the backbone of the Commonwealth of Nations, fostering unity and celebrating diversity among its member countries. Through its programs, initiatives, and collaborative approach, the Secretariat is vital in promoting good governance, human rights, and sustainable development across the Commonwealth and beyond. It serves as a testament to the power of international cooperation in creating a better world for all.

The Commonwealth Games Federation

The Commonwealth Games Federation (CGF) is an international organisation that is vital in promoting unity and diversity among member countries by hosting the Commonwealth Games. Founded in 1930 as the British Empire Games Federation, it has become a symbol of sporting excellence, cultural exchange, and global collaboration.

With a membership of 71 countries from all regions of the Commonwealth, the CGF ensures that the Commonwealth Games are held every four years, bringing together athletes, officials, and spectators from around the world. The Games serve as a platform for athletes to showcase their talents, foster international friendships, and promote peace and understanding.

The CGF aims to create an inclusive environment where athletes compete on a level playing field, regardless of nationality, gender, or background. It upholds the principles of fair play, integrity, and respect, setting high standards for sportsmanship and ethical conduct. By adhering to these values, the CGF cultivates a sense of camaraderie among nations and helps to build a more harmonious world.

In addition to organising the Commonwealth Games, the CGF also undertakes various initiatives to support and develop sports in member countries. It provides financial assistance, training programs, and technical expertise to promote sports participation, especially among youth and marginalised communities. By doing so, the CGF aims to harness the transformative power of sports to improve lives and foster social cohesion.

Furthermore, the CGF encourages cultural exchange and understanding by organising cultural programs alongside the Games. These programs showcase the rich diversity of the Commonwealth, with performances, exhibitions, and events that celebrate the unique memories of countries, art, and heritage of member courses not only promote cultural appreciation but foster a sense of belonging and pride among athletes and spectators.

In conclusion, the Commonwealth Games Federation plays a crucial role in uniting member countries through the power of sport and culture. It strives to create an inclusive and equitable environment where athletes can compete, learn, and grow. By embracing diversity and promoting unity, the CGF exemplifies the values of the Commonwealth and inspires generations to come.

The Commonwealth of Nations

The Commonwealth of Nations, often referred to simply as the Commonwealth, is an intergovernmental organisation comprising 54 member states, all of which are former territories of the British Empire. This is established to foster this unique association cooperation, promote democracy, and advance socio-economic development among its diverse member countries. The Commonwealth Chronicles delves into the tales of this remarkable organisation and diversity within this region. A shared history, language, and legal system binds the Commonwealth with a noteworthy tapestry of cultures and traditions encompassing global countries. From India to Canada, Nigeria to Australia, the Commonwealth embodies the incredible diversity of its member states. This subchapter of the book explores the rich tapestry of the Commonwealth, celebrating its unity in diversity.

One of the most significant aspects of the Commonwealth is its member nations' enduring bond, diverse backgrounds, and shared commitment to democratic ideals, human rights, and the rule of law. Through regular meetings, summits, and forums, member states collaborate on various global challenges, such as climate change, poverty alleviation, and gender equality. The Commonwealth Chronicles presents captivating anecdotes that shed light on the remarkable unity within this diverse group.

Furthermore, the Commonwealth is vital in promoting economic development and trade among its member states. The organisation facilitates economic cooperation, supports sustainable development, and encourages investment in emerging markets. By sharing knowledge, best practices, and resources, the member countries work together to uplift their economies and improve the lives of their citizens. Within the pages of this subchapter, readers will discover inspiring stories of economic transformation and progress within the Commonwealth.

Lastly, the Commonwealth showcases the power of cultural exchange and collaboration through its diverse cultural understanding and appreciation among member countries. From the Commonwealth Youth Program, through its varied range of programs and initiatives, Games, where athletes from various nations compete on a global stage, to the Commonwealth Youth Program, which empowers young leaders, the organisation promotes a sense of shared identity and belonging. This subchapter of the book highlights the heartwarming stories of cultural exchange, artistic collaborations, and educational programs that contribute to the vibrant tapestry of the Commonwealth.

In conclusion, the Commonwealth of Nations is a remarkable organisation that brings together diverse countries united by a shared history and commitment to democracy. The Commonwealth Chronicles explores the tales of unity and diversity within this exceptional organisation, captivating readers with stories of collaboration, economic progress, and cultural exchange. Whether you are a general reader or have a specific interest in the Commonwealth, this subchapter will inspire and inform, shedding light on the powerful impact of unity in diversity.

Chapter 5

Commonwealth Countries: Unity in Diversity

Africa in the Commonwealth

Africa plays a vital role in the Commonwealth, a diverse community of nations united by shared values and a commitment to promoting peace, democracy, and development. With 19 member countries located in different regions of the continent, Africa's presence within the Commonwealth is significant and multifaceted. This subchapter explores the rich histoAfrica's challenges and contributions of Africa without organisation.

Africa's association with the Commonwealth dates back to its colonial past. Many African nations were once under British rule, and upon gaining independence, they chose to maintain their membership in the Commonwealth. This decision reflects the enduring ties between Africa and the other member countries, emphasising the importance of historical connections in fostering unity and cooperation.

Despite the shared history, Africa's diverse cultures, languages, and political systems present unique challenges within the Commonwealth. The subchapter delves into the complexities of governance, economic development, and social progress that African nations face. From the struggles of post-colonial transitions to the ongoing fight against poverty and inequality, Africa's journey within the Commonwealth offers valuable lessons in resilience and determination.

Moreover, the subchapter highlights Africa's contributions to the Commonwealth's overarching goals. African nations have actively participated in various initiatives, programs, and partnerships. They have made significant contributions in areas such as peacekeeping, conflict resolution, and the promotion of human rights. Furthermore, African voices have been instrumental in shaping the Commonwealth's agenda, advocating for climate change, gender equality, and youth empowerment.

Additionally, the subchapter explores the economic potential of Africa within the Commonwealth. With its vast natural resources, burgeoning markets, and a young and dynamic population, Africa presents significant investment opportunities and collaboration opportunities. The C opportunitiesommonwealth provides a platform for African nations to engage with other member countries, fostering economic growth and development.

In conclusion, Africa's presence within the Commonwealth is vital, reflecting a shared history, diverse challenges, and enormous potential. This subchapter sheds light on the non-African nations' experiences and contributions to Recognising the importance of unity and diversity in achieving the Commonwealth's shared goals. By understanding Africa's role within this global organisation, the reader gains insights into the complexities and triumphs of a continent striving for progress and prosperity.

Nigeria: The Giant of Africa

Nigeria, often referred to as the "Giant of Africa, " is a country that embodies the essence of the Commonwealth. Situated in West Africa, it is a nation with a rich cultural heritage, diverse ethnic groups, and a vibrant history. This subchapter in the book "Commonwealth Chronicles: Tales of Unity and Diversity" aims to shed light on Nigeria's significance within the Commonwealth and its unique contributions to the world.

With a population of over 200 million people, Nigeria is the most populous country in Africa. Its vast size and diverse population make it a microcosm of the continent. The nation is home to more than 250 different ethnic groups, each with its distinct language, traditions, and customs. This diversity is celebrated and respected throughout the Commonwealth, as it reflects the unity in diversity that the organisation stands for.

Nigeria's history is intertwined with the struggles and triumphs of the African continent. From the colonial era to its independence in 1960, Nigeria has faced numerous challenges and has emerged as a symbol of resilience. The country's leaders, such as Nnamdi Azikiwe and Obafemi Awolowo, played pivotal roles in the fight for independence and the subsequent development of Nigeria. These stories of courage and determination resonate with Commonwealth nations, as they can draw inspiration from Nigeria's journey towards self-governance.

One of Nigeria's greatest strengths lies in its natural resources. The country is blessed with abundant oil, making it one of the largest oil producers in the world. However, Nigeria's contributions extend beyond the energy sector. It is also known for its vibrant arts and culture scene, producing renowned authors like Chinua Achebe and Wole Soyinka, who have made significant contributions to the literary world. Nigeria's cultural exports, such as music, fashion, and film, have captivated audiences globally and have a source of pride for the Commonwealth; Nigeria plays a vital role as an economic powerhouse and a champion of regional stability. The nation has been actively involved in peacekeeping missions across Africa, showcasing its commitment to maintaining peace and security in the region.

Furthermore, Nigeria's strong economy and entrepreneurial spirit have made it an attractive destination for investment and trade within the Commonwealth.

In conclusion, Nigeria's significance within the Commonwealth cannot be overstated. As the Giant of Africa, it embodies the values of unity and diversity celebrated throughout the organisation. Its rich cultural heritage, diverse population, and contributions to various sectors make Nigeria a country that inspires and influences the Commonwealth and the world.

South Africa: From Apartheid to Democracy

South Africa's journey from apartheid to democracy is a remarkable story of resilience, courage, and triumph over adversity. In the pages of history, this chapter stands out as a testament to the power of unity and the indomitable spirit of the South African people. From the dark days of apartheid to the dawn of democracy, South Africa's transformation inspires the Commonwealth.

Apartheid, a system of racial segregation and discrimination, plagued South Africa for nearly five decades. Under this oppressive regime, the majority of the population, particularly the black African population, was denied fundamental human rights and subjected to brutal discrimination. However, the determination for change grew, fueled by the voices of activists such as Nelson Mandela, Desmond Tutu, and countless others who championed the cause of justice and equality.

The turning point came in 1994 when South Africa held its first democratic elections. This historic event marked the end of apartheid and the birth of a new era. Nelson Mandela, the iconic leader who had spent 27 years in prison for his fight against apartheid, became the country's first black president. His inauguration represented South Africa and the Commonwealth, a testament to the power of unity and the shared values of democracy and equality.

The transition from apartheid to democracy was not without its challenges. Reconciliation and healing were essential to building a united South Africa, as the wounds of the past ran deep. The Truth and

Reconciliation Commission, established to investigate human rights abuses during the apartheid era, played a crucial role in this process. It provided a platform for victims and perpetrators to share their stories and seek forgiveness, promoting a culture of forgiveness and understanding.

Since then, South Africa has made significant strides towards building a more inclusive society. The country has implemented progressive policies to bridge the racial and economic divide, promoting education, healthcare, and economic opportunities for all citizens. While challenges remain, South Africa's journey serves as a beacon of hope for the Commonwealth, reminding us of the transformative power of unity, diversity, and democracy.

In conclusion, South Africa's transition from apartheid to democracy is a powerful testament to the resilience and strength of its people. This chapter in the Commonwealth Chronicles highlights the significance of unity and diversity in overcoming the darkest periods of history. It is a story that resonates with people from all walks of life, inspiring us never to lose hope and to always strive for a world where justice, equality, and democracy prevail.

Asia in the Commonwealth

Asia, the world's largest and most populous continent, has played a significant role in the Commonwealth since its establishment. The Commonwealth, an intergovernmental organisation formed in 1931, aims to promote peace, democracy, and development among its member countries. With diverse languages and traditions, Asia brings a unique flavour to the Commonwealth, enriching its unity and diversity.

The presence of Asian countries in the Commonwealth is notable, with India being one of its founding members. India's journey from being a colony under British rule to becoming an independent nation is a testament to the power of unity and the values upheld by the Commonwealth. Today, India stands as one of the largest democracies in the world, showcasing the success of democratic principles promoted by the Commonwealth.

Apart from India, other Asian countries, including Pakistan, Bangladesh, Malaysia, and Singapore, are active members of the Commonwealth. With their distinct histories and contributions, these nations contribute to the diverse organisation's tapestry of ideas and perspectives within the Commonwealth, bringing together these nations from East Asia to South Asia, the Cre experiences, exchange knowledge, and foster cooperation in various fields.

The Commonwealth has been instrumental in promoting sustainable development and addressing challenges Asian countries face. Member nations receive support in education, healthcare, and infrastructure development through initiatives such as the Commonwealth Fund for Technical Cooperation. This assistance has been crucial in uplifting communities and empowering individuals, particularly in rural and marginalised regions.

Furthermore, Asia's economic growth and technological advancements have made it an essential player in the global arena. The Commonwealth provides a platform for Asian nations to collaborate with other member countries to harness these advancements for the benefit of all. The sharing of resources facilitates trade, investment, and innovation, leading to mutual growth and prosperity.

Asia's rich cultural heritage also finds expression within the Commonwealth. From diverse art forms, traditional music, and cuisines to vibrant festivals and religious celebrations, Asian cultures bring a sense of vibrancy to the organisation. The Commonwealth Games, a multi-sport event held every four years, showcases the sporting prowess of Asian nations, fostering friendly competition and cultural exchange.

In conclusion, Asia's presence in the Commonwealth is significant and valuable. The continent's contributions in terms of history, diversity, and development have enriched the organisation, fostering unity among its members. Through collaboration and mutual support, the Commonwealth promotes peace, democracy, and sustainable growth in Asia and beyond, ensuring a brighter future for all its member countries.

India: The Largest Democracy

India, the land of vibrant cultures, ancient traditions, and diverse languages, stands proudly as the largest democracy in the worThisthis subcha, we will delve into the uniIndia's democratic journey of Indilore and the key aspects that make it a shining example of unity amidst diversity.

With its rich history dating back thousands of years, India has witnessed the rise and fall of numerous empires and kingdoms. However, when India gained independence from British colonial rule, the foundation of its democratic principles was laid. The Constitution of India, adopted in 1950, established a robust framework for governance, emphasising the values of liberty, equality, and fraternity.

One of the remarkable features of Indian democracy is its sheer size and diversity. Home to over 1. 3 billion people speaking more than 1, 600 languages and practising various religions, India showcases a tapestry of cultures that coexist harmoniously. The democratic system in India ensures that every citizen, regardless of their background, has a voice in shaping the nation's future. From the snow-capped peaks of the Himalayas to the serene backwaters of Kerala, every region and community contributes to the vibrant tapestry of Indian democracy.

India's democratic process is based on a multi-tiered system, with elections at various levels – from the national parliament to state assemblies and local bodies. The world's largest democratic exercise, the general elections, witnesses millions of voters casting their ballots, ensuring that the government represents their aspirations. Political parties representing diverse ideologies and interests compete spirally, fostering healthy debates and discussions.

Furthermore, India's democratic fabric is strengthened by a free and independent press, which plays a pivotal role in holding power accountable and promoting transparency. The media acts as a watchdog, ensuring that the voices of the marginalised are heard and empowering citizens with information.

The Commonwealth, a voluntary association of countries sharing historical ties with the British Empire, has significantly promoted principles across its member nations. As a proud member of the Commonwealth, India actively participates in various programs and initiatives aimed at strengthening democratic institutions, promoting good governance, and fostering mutual understanding among member countries.

In conclusion, India's journey as the largest democracy in the world is a testament to the power of unity amidst diversity. Its democratic principles, enshrined in the Constitution, have paved the way for a vibrant and inclusive society. As we embark on exploremmonwealth Chronicles, let us marvel at India's democratic spirit, where every citizen's voice matters and diversity thrives.

Malaysia: A Multicultural Nation

Malaysia, a vibrant and diverse Southeast Asian country, is a shining example of a multicultural nation within the Commonwealth. Known for its rich cultural heritage, the country is a melting pot of various ethnicities, religions, and traditions, making it a unique and fascinating place to explore.

One of the critical elements that define Malaysia is its multicultural society. The nation has three main ethnic groups: Malays, Chinese, and Indians. Each group has its distinct language, customs, and traditions, creating a colourful tapestry of diversity. Malaysians take great pride in their multicultural identity, and this unity in diversity has significantly shaped the country's history, arts, and cuisine.

Malaysia's history reflects the influences of various cultures. The Malay kingdom was among the earliest civilisations in the region, and its rich heritage can be seen in the architecture and traditions passed down through generations. The Chinese community, which migrated to Malaysia centuries ago, brought their language, cuisine, and customs, which have become an integral part of Malaysian culture. Similarly, the Indian community has made immense contributions to the nation's cultural fabric through its vibrant festivals, music, and dance forms.

Religion is another crucial aspect of Malaysia's multiculturalism. Islam is the official religion, followed by Buddhism, Hinduism, and Christianity. Despite the dominance of Islam, religious freedom is guaranteed, and people of all faiths coexist harmoniously. This religious diversity is most evident during festive seasons such as Eid, Chinese New Year, Diwali, and Christmas, when the entire nation comes together to celebrate, irrespective of their religious beliefs.

Malaysia's multiculturalism extends beyond just its people; it is evident in its cuisine. The fusion of flavours from Malay, Chinese, and Indian cuisines has given birth to a unique culinary experience. Whether it's the spicy and aromatic Nasi Lemak, the savoury Char Kway Teow, or the mouthwatering Chicken Biryani, Malaysia offers a gastronomic adventure that tantalises the taste buds of locals and visitors alike.

In conclusion, Malaysia is a shining example of a multicultural nation within the Commonwealth. Its diverse ethnic groups, rich history, harmonious religious coexistence, and fusion cuisine make it a fascinating destination for anyone seeking to explore the beauty of unity in diversity. Whether wandering through the bustling streets of Kuala Lumpur, savouring the mouthwatering street food, or immersing yourself in the vibrant festivals, Malaysia will leave a lasting impression on visitors from all walks of life.

Europe in the Commonwealth

Europe plays a significant role within the Commonwealth, a diverse and united group of nations that spans the globe. As we delve into the subchapter "Europe in the Commonwealth" within the book "Commonwealth Chronicles: Tales of Unity and Diversity, " we explore the European countries' relationship and contributions to international organisations. This content aims to provide a comprehensive overview for a general audience, specifically focusing on those interested in the Commonwealth.

With its history and cultural diversity, Europe has made invaluable contributions to the Commonwealth. Many European countries, including the United Kingdom, Malta, and Cyprus, are full members, while others, such as Belgium and Germany, hold associate membership. These nations have actively participated in the nation's identity and promoted the values of democracy, human rights, and sustainable development.

One of the most prominent European Commonwealth members is the United Kingdom. With its historical ties to many Commonwealth nations, the UK has played a pivotal role in the organisation's development. The British monarchy also serves as the symbolic head of the Commonwealth, reinforcing the unity and shared heritage among member countries.

Another European nation that has made significant contributions is Malta. As a small island nation in the Mediterranean, Malta holds a unique position within the Commonwealth. It has actively promoted dialogue, cooperation, and cultural exchange among member states by hosting the biennial Commonwealth Heads of Government Meeting (CHOGM).

Cyprus, a Strategic location bridging Europe, Africa, and Asia, has also played a crucial role in the Commonwealth. It has utilised its position to foster economic cooperation, regional stability, and cultural understanding within the organisation. The ComBaseddon has a worthy Commonwealth Secretariat that works closely with Cyprus to promote these objectives and enhance the Commonwealth's presence in Europe.

Furthermore, associate member countries like Belgium and Germany have strengthened the relationship between Europe and the Commonwealth. These nations have facilitated closer ties and mutual understanding between European and Commonwealth countries through their participation in various Commonwealth programs and initiatives.

Europe's involvement in the Commonwealth underscores the organisation's commitment to inclusivity and diversity. BrinThewealth creates a platform for dialogue, cooperation, and shared progress. By bringing together nations from different continents' historical, cultural, and political influences within the Commonwealth, Europ continues to shape the organisation's future, ensuring it remains a relevant and dynamic force in the modern world.

In conclusion, the subchapter "Europe in the Commonwealth" comprehensively explores the contributions and significance of European countries within this international organisation. From the United Kingdom's historical ties to Malta's hosting of CHOGM and the active participation of associate member countries like Belgium and Germany, Europe plays a vital role in shaping the Commonwealth's identity and promoting its core values. By fostering dialogue, cooperation, and cultural exchange, Europe strengthens the unity and diversity of the Commonwealth, making it a truly global entity.

United Kingdom: The Birthplace of the Commonwealth

The United Kingdom holds a significant place in the history of the Commonwealth, serving as its birthplace and playing a crucial role in its evolution over the years. The Commonwealth, also known as the Commonwealth of Nations, is an intergovernmental organisation comprising 54 member countries, most of which are former territories of the British Empire. In this subchapter, we delve into the rich history and enduring influence of the United Kingdom on the Commonwealth.

The formation of the Commonwealth can be traced back to the London Declaration of 1949, which established the modern framework of the organisation. However, its roots can be found in the British Empire, which, at its height, encompassed a vast global network of territories under British rule. The United Kingdom's colonial legacy left impacted territories, shaping their culture, governance, and legal systems.

The United Kingdom's pivotal role in the Commonwealth is evident in various aspects, including its ongoing support for the organisation's principles and initiatives. The British monarch, currently Queen Elizabeth II, serves as the symbolic figurehead of the Commonwealth, emphasising the historical ties that unite member countries. AdditioThewealth Secretariat, the organisation's administrative body, is based in London, further highlighting the UK's central role.

The United Kingdom's commitment to promoting unity and diversity within the Commonwealth is exemplified through various initiatives. The Commonwealth Games, a multi-sport event held every four years, brings together athletes from member countries to compete globally. This event fosters friendly competition, cultural exchange, and understanding among nations.

Furthermore, the United Kingdom actively supports development projects. It provides aid to Commonwealth countries, particularly those facing economic challenges—through the means to empower member nations through partnerships and collaborations to ensure their socio-economic development.

Despite the United Kingdom's historical ties with the Commonwealth, the organisation has evolved into a diverse and inclusive entity transcending its colonial origins. Today, member countries represent various regions, cultures, and religions, united by a shared commitment to democratic values, human rights, and sustainable development.

In conclusion, the United Kingdom's role as the birthplace of the Commonwealth cannot be understated. Its historical ties, ongoing support, and commitment to unity and diversity have shaped the organisation into what it is today. The Commonwealth stands as a testament to the shafts member countries' values and aspirations together to promote peace, prosperity, and mutual understanding on a global scale.

Malta: The Mediterranean Jewel

Nestled in the heart of the Mediterranean Sea, the tiny island nation of Malta shines as a true gem of the region. Known for its rich history, stunning landscapes, and vibrant culture, this Mediterranean jewel offers a unique experience to visitors from around the world. As a member of the Commonwealth, Malta holds a special place within the global community, fostering unity and diversity in its distinct way.

Steeped in history, Malta boasts a captivating past that can be traced back thousands of years. From the ancient temples of Ħaġar Qim and Mnajdra, older than the Egyptian pyramids, to the magnificent medieval city of Mdina, the island is a living testament to the civilisations that graced its shores. Visitors can immerse themselves in the stories of the Knights Hospitaller, who left an indelible mark on the architecture and culture of Malta or explore the underground tunnels of the capital city, Valletta, which played a pivotal role during World War II. The island's history is a tapestry woven with tales of conquest, resilience, and cultural exchange.

Beyond its historical significance, Malta offers a breathtaking natural beauty that captivates the senses. The azure waters surrounding the island beckon travellers to explore their depths through diving or snorkelling, revealing a vibrant underwater world teeming with colourful marine life and ancient shipwrecks. The rugged cliffs and hidden coves along its coastline offer a picturesque backdrop for leisurely walks or tranquil boat rides. Inland, visitors can wander through rolling hills adorned with quaint villages, vineyards, and olive groves, soaking in the Mediterranean sunshine and the island's laid-back charm.

Malta's cultural diversity is another facet that sets it apart. As a member of the Commonwealth, the nation embraces its multicultural heritage, fostering an environment of inclusivity and understanding. Visitors can witness this diversity through the various festivals, art exhibitions, and culinary experiences that celebrate the island's mix of influences, including Arabic, Italian, British, and African. Whether indulging in the local delicacies, exploring the vibrant street markets, or engaging with the warm-hearted locals, travellers will immerse themselves in a kaleidoscope of flavours, sights, and sounds that make Malta unique.

In conclusion, Malta is a Mediterranean jewel that shines brightly within the Commonwealth. Its rich history, stunning landscapes, and vibrant culture make it a must-visit destination for travellers seeking a truly immersive experience. From exploring ancient temples to diving into crystal-clear waters, Malta offers various attractions that cater to all interests. As visitors journey to this island nation, they will be welcomed into a tapestry of unity and diversity, where the past and present intertwine to create an unforgettable experience.

Oceania in the Commonwealth

The Commonwealth, an association of nations bound by shared values and a commitment to democracy, has a rich and diverse membership that spans the globe. One of its most vibrant and culturally diverse regions is Oceania, which comprises thousands of islands across the vast Pacific Ocean. This subchapter explores the unique contributions and challenges Oceania faces within the Commonwealth.

Oceania boasts a remarkable tapestry of cultures, languages, and traditions. ThOceania is a mosaic of identities from the igneous peoples of Australia and New Zealand to the vibrant communities in Fiji, Papua New Guinea, and the Pacific island nations. Ocean's diverse cultural heritages enrich the Commonwealth and provide a platform for understanding and appreciating the beauty of human diversity.

The Commonwealth plays a significant role in supporting Oceania's nations as they tackle common challenges such as climate change, economic development, and social inclusion. Oceania's vulnerability to rising sea levels, extreme weather events, and the depletion of marine resources necessitates collaborative efforts to mitigate and adapt to these environmental threats. The Commonwealth's shared commitment to sustainable development and climate action provides Oceania with a platform to advocate for its unique concerns on the global stage.

Furthermore, the Commonwealth promotes economic cooperation and trade within Oceania. Through various initiatives such as the Pacific Trade Invest and the Pacific Regional Trade and Development Facility, the Commonwealth helps Oceania's nations harness their economic potential and overcome barriers to market access. FostThewealth empowers Oceania's communities to create sustainable livelihoods and reduce poverty.

Despi by fostering economic development the numerous advantages of Oceania's Commonwealth membership, the region faces specific challenges. Limited access to healthcare, education, and essential services in remote island communities remains a pressing issue. The Commonwealth recognises these disparities and works collaboratively with Oceania's governments and civil society to address them. Initiatives like the Commonwealth Health Hub and the Commonwealth Education Trust provide resources, expertise, and funding to improve healthcare and education outcomes across Oceania.

In conclusion, Oceania's vibrant cultures, environmental challenges, and unique socio-economic needs make it a significant and valued member of the Commonwealth. The Commonwealth seeks to empower Oceania's nations and communities through collaboration, ensuring their voices are heard and their needs addressed. By celebrating unity in diversity, the Commonwealth embraces Oceania's rich heritage and champions its aspirations for a prosperous and sustainable future.

Australia: The Land Down Under

Australia, the Land Down Under, is a vast and diverse country in the southern hemisphere. The world's sixth-largest country encompasses many landscapes, from stunning coastlines to rugged mountain ranges and vast deserts. As a member of the Commonwealth, Australia holds a unique position in the global community, characterised by unity and diversity.

One of the defining features of Australia is its multicultural society. With a rich indigenous history dating back over 65, 000 years, Australia has become a melting pot of different cultures and ethnicities. The Aboriginal and Torres Strait Islander peoples, the country's first inhabitants, have a deep connection to the land and have contributed immensely to Australia's cultural heritage.

The arrival of European settlers in the late 18th century brought a wave of diversity to the continent. Waves of immigration from Europe, Asia, and other parts of the world have shaped Australia's population and cultural landscape. Today, Australia is a multicultural society that celebrates diversity and promotes inclusivity.

Australia's natural wonders are equally diverse. From the iconic Great Barrier Reef, one of the world's most remarkable natural wonders, to the vast Outback, home to unique wildlife like kangaroos and emus, Australia is a land of breathtaking beauty. Its national parks, such as Kakadu and Uluru-Kata Tjuta, showcase the country's rich biodiversity and offer countless opportunities for exploration and adventure.

In addition to its natural beauty, Australia is also known for its vibrant cities. Sydney, Withonic Opera House and Harbour Bridge is a buSydney-styling metropolis that combines modernity with laid-back beach culture. Melbourne, on the other hand, is renowned for its thriving arts scene and diverse culinary experiences. Other cities like Brisbane, Perth, and Adelaide offer their unique blend of cultural attractions and urban lifestyles.

Australia's membership in the Commonwealth further strengthens its ties with other countries that, with a British colonial rule history association, ensure unity and cooperation among member countries, fostering diplomatic relations, trade, and cultural exchanges.

In conclusion, Australia, the Land Down Under, is a country of remarkable diversity and unity. Its multicultural society, breathtaking landscapes, and vibrant cities make it a truly unique destination. Whether exploring the Great Barrier Reef, hiking through the Outback, or immersing yourself in the cultural hub of Sydney, Australia offers an unforgettable experience for locals and visitors alike. As a proud member of the Commonwealth, Australia stands as a testament to the power of unity amidst diversity.

Fiji: A Tropical Paradise

As the sun rises over the turquoise waters of the South Pacific, a tropical paradise beckons visitors worldwide to the enchanting islands of Fiji. Nestled within the Commonwealth, this archipelago is a true gem that blends unity and diversity, offering a unique experience to all who venture here.

The islands of Fiji boast a vibrant cultural tapestry, reflecting the harmonious coexistence of its indigenous Melanesian people and the Indian settlers who arrived during the colonial era. This fusion of traditions is evident in the local cuisine, where flavours from both cultures intertwine to create a compelling gastronomic adventure. From the earthy flavours of traditional Fijian dishes like Kokoda, a marinated raw fish salad, to the aromatic spices of Indian-inspired curries, every bite in Fiji celebrates its rich diversity.

Beyond its cultural heritage, Fiji is renowned for its breathtaking natural beauty. Pristine white sandy beaches stretch as far as the eye can see, fringed by swaying coconut palms and lush tropical vegetation. The warm waters teem with vibrant marine life, beckoning snorkelers and divers to explore its colourful coral reefs. The islands also have majestic waterfalls, hidden caves, and remote hiking trails that glimpse Fiji's untouched wilderness.

In addition to its idyllic landscapes, Fiji is famous for its warm and welcoming people. Fijians, known for their genuine hospitality, greet visitors with open arms, inviting them to immerse themselves in the local way of life. Whether participating in a traditional Kava ceremony, where a ceremonial drink is shared or joining in the lively dances and music during a Fijian make performance, visitors are embraced as part of the community and encouraged to forge lasting connections.

While Fiji embraces its traditional roots, it also offers modern amenities and luxurious accommodations. From exclusive resorts nestled on private islands to eco-friendly boutique hotels, there is an array of options to suit every traveller's preferences and budget. Whether you seek relaxation on pristine beaches or thrilling adventures like zip-lining through lush rainforests, Fiji has something for everyone.

In conclusion, Fiji is a tropical paradise that showcases the beauty of unity and diversity within the Commonwealth. Its rich cultural heritage, stunning natural landscapes, and warm hospitality make it a must-visit destination for travellers seeking a memorable experience. So, pack your bags, embrace the spirit of aloha, and let Fiji enchant you with its irresistible charm.

The Americas in the Commonwealth

The Americas, a vast and diverse landmass comprising North, Central, and South America, have a rich and colourful history within the Commonwealth. This subchapter delves into the unique experiences, challenges, and contributions of the Americas to the global community of nations.

Stretching from the Arctic Circle to the southern tip of Patagonia, the Americas boast a staggering array of cultures, languages, and landscapes. From the towering skyscrapers of New York City to the ancient ruins of Machu Picchu, the region holds a treasure trove of wonders waiting to be explored.

One of the Americas' most notable contributions to the Commonwealth is its rich cultural heritage. Indigenous peoples have inhabited the lands for thousands of years, leaving behind a legacy of art, music, and traditions that continue to shape the fabric of society. From the vibrant celebrations of Carnival in Brazil to the powwows of Native American tribes, the Americas offer a kaleidoscope of customs that celebrate unity in diversity.

The Americas have also played a pivotal role in shaping the political landscape of the Commonwealth. The United States, with its founding principles of liberty and democracy, has served as a beacon of inspiration for other nations striving for independence and self-governance. Canada, known for its commitment to multiculturalism and inclusivity, has paved the way for peaceful coexistence among diverse communities.

Economically, the Americas have been vital contributors to the Commonwealth. The United States and Canada are among the world's largest economies, with bustling trade networks and technological advancements that have revolutionised industries. Meanwhile, countries such as Brazil and Mexico have emerged as economic powerhouses in their respective regions, fueling innovation and growth.

However, the Americas have not been immune to challenges. Social inequalities, political unrest, and environmental issues have plagued the region, posing significant obstacles to progress. Yet, the resilience of its people and the spirit of cooperation within the Commonwealth have helped navigate these difficulties, fostering unity and progress.

In conclusion, the Americas are integral to the Commonwealth, offering a rich tapestry of cultures, a strong political influence, and dynamic economies. Despite the challenges, the region strives for unity, diversity, and progress. By celebrating and embracing the

Americas' contributions, we can strengthen the bonds of the Commonwealth and foster a brighter future for all its members.

Canada: A Mosaic of Cultures

Canada, often called a "mosaic of cultures, " is a shining example of unity and diversity within the Commonwealth. As one of the world's largest and most diverse countries, it is home to many cultures, languages, and traditions. This subchapter explores Canadian society's rich tapestry, highlighting the harmonious coexistence of various ethnicities and the celebration of multiculturalism.

Situated in North America, Canada has been shaped by its historical ties to Europe and indigenous peoples. The country's multicultural identity began with the arrival of European settlers and continues to evolve with the influx of immigrants from around the globe. The Commonwealth, with its shared history and values, plays a significant role in fostering cultural exchange and understanding between Canada and its fellow member nations.

Canada's multiculturalism policy, established in 1971, has been instrumental in promoting diversity and inclusivity. This policy recognises that cultural differences should be embraced rather than assimilated, allowing individuals to maintain their unique identities while contributing to the overall fabric of Canadian society. As a result, Canada has become a haven for those seeking a better life and equal opportunities, creating a harmonious blend of cultures that enriches the nation as a whole.

The mosaic of cultures in Canada is reflected in its vibrant cities, where one can experience the sights, sounds, and flavours of various ethnic communities. Toronto, for instance, is known as one of the most multicultural cities in the world, with over 200 ethnic groups calling it home. From Chinatown to Little Italy, each neighbourhood showcases the distinct heritage of its residents, contributing to the multicultural tapestry that defines Canada.

Furthermore, Canada's commitment to cultural diversity extends beyond its urban centres. Indigenous cultures, representing the land's original inhabitants, are deeply rooted in the country's identity. Canada strives to acknowledge and rectify past injustices through various initiatives, such as the Truth and Reconciliation Commission, fostering greater understanding and appreciation for indigenous traditions.

In conclusion, Canada's multiculturalism and its place within the Commonwealth exemplify the strength and beauty of diversity. The country's commitment to inclusivity allows individuals from all walks of life to contribute to its rich tapestry of cultures. As a beacon of unity and acceptance, Canada inspires other Commonwealth nations, demonstrating the potential for a harmonious coexistence of diverse ethnicities. Whether exploring its vibrant cities or experiencing indigenous traditions, Canada continues to embrace its multicultural heritage, making it a true mosaic of cultures within the Commonwealth.

Jamaica: The Reggae Nation

Jamaica, the vibrant island nation nestled in the Caribbean Sea, holds a special place in the hearts of music enthusiasts worldwide. Jamaica has captivated the global imagination, from its breathtaking natural beauty to its rich cultural heritage. However, the island's unique contribution to the world of music, mainly Reggae, has earned it the title "The Reggae Nation. "

With its distinctive beats and soulful lyrics, Reggae has become synonymous with Jamaica and its people. Born out of the vibrant streets of Kingston in the 1960s, reggae music served as a powerful medium of expression for the marginalised communities of Jamaica. It became a voice for the voiceless, addressing social and political injustices and spreading messages of love, peace, and unity.

One cannot discuss Reggae without mentioning the legendary Bob Marley, the undisputed king of Reggae. His iconic songs such as "One Love, " "No Woman, No Cry, " and "Redemption Song" continue to resonate with audiences worldwide, transcending cultural and linguistic barriers. Marley's music embodies the spirit of Jamaica, blending themes of spirituality, social consciousness, and love for humanity.

Beyond Bob Marley, Jamaica has produced many talented reggae artists who have significantly contributed to the genre. Artists such as Peter Tosh, Jimmy Cliff, Toots and the Maytals, and Buju Banton have left an indelible mark on reggae music, each with their unique style and message. Today, the reggae scene in Jamaica continues to thrive, with new talents emerging and carrying the torch forward.

Reggae's influence extends far beyond the shores of Jamaica. Its infectious rhythms and uplifting messages have inspired countless artists across the globe, leading to the creation of various subgenres such as reggae fusion, dancehall, and dub. Reggae festivals and concerts draw music enthusiasts from all walks of life, fostering a sense of unity and celebration of diversity.

Jamaica's musical legacy is deeply intertwined with its cultural heritage, reflecting its people's resilience, creativity, and indomitable spirit. The reggae nation serves as a shining example of the power of music to transcend boundaries and bring people together. Whether you're a casual listener or a die-hard reggae fan, visiting Jamaica will be a transformative experience, immersing you in the soul-stirring rhythms and infectious energy that define the reggae nation.

In conclusion, Jamaica's reggae music is a cultural phenomenon that has resonated with people worldwide. Its powerful messages of love, unity, and social justice inspire and uplift generations. The reggae nation stands as a testament to the rich diversity and unity found in the Commonwealth, showcasing its people's remarkable talents and contributions.

Chapter 6

Commonwealth Achievements and Challenges

Advancements in Education and Healthcare

Education and healthcare are two fundamental pillars that shape the progress and well-being of any society. These sectors have witnessed significant advancements in the Commonwealth, fostering unity and diversity among member countries. This subchapter explores the remarkable achievements and innovations in education and healthcare that have transformed the lives of individuals and communities across the Commonwealth.

Education has always been considered the key to unlocking opportunities and empowering individuals. In the Commonwealth, concerted efforts have been made to improve access to quality education for all. Establishing numerous educational institutions and implementing innovative teaching methods have ensured that knowledge reaches even the most remote corners of member countries.

One aspect that has revolutionised education is the integration of technology. With the advent of digital platforms, students can access various educational resources from anywhere, breaking down geographical barriers. Online learning platforms, interactive e-books, and virtual classrooms have become commonplace, providing flexibility and personalised learning experiences.

Moreover, the Commonwealth has recognised the importance of promoting diversity and inclusivity in education. Efforts have been made to incorporate diverse cultural perspectives, history, and languages into the curriculum. This approach celebrates the unique heritage of member countries and fosters a sense of unity and understanding among students from different cultural backgrounds.

In healthcare, the Commonwealth has made remarkable progress in improving the quality and accessibility of healthcare services. Advanced medical technologies, groundbreaking research, and collaboration among member countries have led to significant disease prevention, diagnosis, and treatment breakthroughs.

Telemedicine has emerged as a game-changer, especially for remote areas with limited access to healthcare facilities. Through telemedicine, patients can receive medical consultations, diagnoses, and even treatment remotely, minimising the need for travel and ensuring timely healthcare interventions.

Furthermore, the Commonwealth has prioritised the development of primary healthcare systems, focusing on preventive measures and community-based care. This approach has significantly reduced the prevalence of infectious diseases, improved maternal and child health, and enhanced overall well-being in member countries.

In conclusion, the Commonwealth has witnessed tremendous advancements in education and healthcare, resulting in improved opportunities and well-being for its diverse population. The integration of technology, emphasis on inclusivity, and focus on preventive healthcare measures have played pivotal roles in transforming these sectors. As the Commonwealth strives for progress and unity, education and healthcare will remain at the forefront, ensuring a brighter and healthier future for all its member countries.

Economic Cooperation and Trade

In the grand tapestry of nations, economic cooperation and trade serve as the threads that weave the fabric of the Commonwealth. The diverse nations that form this esteemed alliance have come together to embrace the spirit of unity, fostering economic growth, resilience, and prosperity. In this subchapter of "Commonwealth Chronicles: Tales of Unity and Diversity, " we explore the pivotal role economic cooperation and trade play in shaping the destiny of this remarkable community.

The Commonwealth is a testament to the power of collaboration and shared goals. With member countries spread across six continents, the potential for economic partnerships and trade opportunities is vast. By leveraging their collective strengths,

Commonwealth nations have forged deep bonds that drive economic growth and development. These nations have created an environment conducive to innovation, entrepreneurship, and sustainable economic progress through open markets, fair trade policies, and investment initiatives.

Trade within the Commonwealth is an intricate web of connections that transcends borders, cultures, and traditions. From the bustling markets of India to the vibrant trade routes of Africa and the Pacific Islands, the exchange of goods and services fuels economic engines and uplifts communities. By embracing the principles of free trade, member countries promote a level playing field, enabling businesses to thrive and consumers to benefit from a wide array of affordable products.

Furthermore, economic cooperation within the Commonwealth extends beyond mere trade. It encompasses a broader spectrum of collaborative initiatives, including capacity building, knowledge sharing, and technological advancements. By pooling resources, expertise, and experiences, member countries can address common challenges like poverty, inequality, and climate change. This collective effort enhances economic resilience and fosters a sense of belonging and shared responsibility among nations.

The Commonwealth's commitment to economic cooperation and trade has yielded remarkable results. GDP growth rates have surged, poverty levels have decreased, and social welfare has improved. However, challenges remain, and it is through continued collaboration that these obstacles can be overcome. By embracing inclusive trade policies, promoting sustainable development, and investing in human capital, the Commonwealth can forge a prosperous future where no member nation is left behind.

In conclusion, economic cooperation and trade form the lifeblood of the Commonwealth. Member countries have built a resilient financial ecosystem that benefits all through a shared commitment to open markets, fair trade, and collaborative initiatives. The tales of unity and diversity within the Commonwealth Chronicles are not just stories; they are the lived experiences of nations united by a common purpose. Together, we can continue to write a narrative of growth, progress, and shared prosperity, ensuring a brighter future for the Commonwealth and its people.

Environmental Conservation and Sustainability

In today's fast-paced and interconnected world, the need for environmental conservation and sustainability has become more critical than ever. With the growing threats of climate change, deforestation, air and water pollution, and the depletion of natural resources, we must take immediate action to protect our planet for future generations.

This subchapter of "Commonwealth Chronicles: Tales of Unity and Diversity" aims to provide a comprehensive overview of environmental conservation and sustainability practices within the context of the Commonwealth. Whether you are a concerned individual, a policymaker, or a member of the Commonwealth, this chapter will equip you with the knowledge and tools necessary to impact the environment positively.

First and foremost, we will explore the concept of environmental conservation and why it is essential for the Commonwealth. We will delve into the interconnectedness of ecosystems, highlighting the ripple effect ecological degradation can have on local communities and global well-being. By understanding the value of biodiversity and the delicate balance of nature, we can appreciate the urgency of preserving our natural resources.

Next, we will delve into sustainable development practices that promote harmony between economic growth and environmental stewardship. We will examine successful case studies from various commonwealth nations, showcasing innovative approaches to renewable energy, waste management, and sustainable agriculture. These examples will inspire and empower readers to adopt similar strategies in their communities.

Furthermore, we will address the role of individuals in environmental conservation and sustainability. From small lifestyle changes, such as reducing waste and conserving water, to advocating for policy reforms, every action counts. We can create a powerful movement for change within the Commonwealth by encouraging personal responsibility and collective effort.

Lastly, this subchapter will highlight the importance of international cooperation and collaboration in tackling global environmental challenges. We will discuss the Commonwealth's role in fostering dialogue and sharing best practices among member nations. We can amplify our efforts through partnerships and knowledge exchange and create a more sustainable future for all.

In conclusion, "Environmental Conservation and Sustainability" is a vital subchapter within "Commonwealth Chronicles: Tales of Unity and Diversity. " Understanding the significance of environmental conservation, adopting sustainable development practices, promoting individual responsibility, and fostering international collaboration can pave the way towards a greener and more sustainable commonwealth. Together, we can protect our precious natural resources and ensure a better tomorrow for generations to come.

Tackling Global Issues: Climate Change, Poverty, and Inequality

In today's interconnected world, where the challenges we face transcend national borders, it is crucial to address pressing global issues collectively. Climate change, poverty, and inequality are among the most significant challenges we face as part of the international Commonwealth. The Commonwealth Chronicles: Tales of Unity and Diversity aims to shed light on these issues and inspire action among individuals, communities, and nations.

Climate change is a threat that affects every corner of the globe, regardless of borders or socio-economic status. Rising temperatures, extreme weather events, and melting ice caps are just a few of the alarming consequences. By exploring the stories of individuals impacted by climate change, this subchapter aims to raise awareness and promote sustainable practices to mitigate its effects.

Poverty and inequality are deeply intertwined, and they persist in both developed and developing Commonwealth countries. This subchapter delves into the stories of those living in poverty, shedding light on the root causes and consequences of such disparities. From examining the impact of unequal access to education and healthcare to exploring strategies for poverty alleviation, this section aims to ignite compassion and drive change.

The Commonwealth, with its diverse member nations, presents a unique platform for collective action. This subchapter highlights successful initiatives and collaborations within the Commonwealth that have addressed these global issues. It showcases how nations have united to share knowledge, resources, and best practices, fostering unity and solidarity in adversity.

Moreover, this subchapter emphasises the importance of individual action. Each of us has a role in tackling climate change, poverty, and inequality. We can collectively make a difference by promoting sustainable lifestyles, responsible consumption, and supporting social justice initiatives. The Commonwealth Chronicles seeks to inspire readers to take action in their own lives and communities, fostering a sense of global citizenship.

In conclusion, the subchapter "Tackling Global Issues: Climate Change, Poverty, and Inequality" explores the urgent challenges we face as part of the global Commonwealth. This chapter aims to inspire unity and diversity in addressing these global issues by sharing stories, highlighting successful initiatives, and encouraging individual action. We can create a more sustainable, equitable, and prosperous future for all.

Chapter 7

Commonwealth Cultural Exchanges and Festivals

Commonwealth Literature and Literary Festivals

Literature has always been a powerful tool for bringing people together and transcending geographical boundaries and cultural differences. In the vast tapestry of literary traditions, Commonwealth literature stands out as a unique genre that celebrates the diverse voices and experiences of the countries belonging to the Commonwealth of Nations. This subchapter explores the rich heritage of Commonwealth literature and the vibrant literary festivals that showcase its beauty and diversity.

Commonwealth literature encompasses the literary works produced by authors from the member countries of the Commonwealth, including countries such as India, Nigeria,

Canada, Australia, and many others. These works reflect the shared historical, political, and cultural experiences of these nations while also highlighting the distinctiveness of each country's literary tradition. From the magical realism of Gabriel Garcia Marquez to the poignant storytelling of Chinua Achebe, Commonwealth literature offers myriad perspectives and narratives that captivate readers worldwide.

Literary festivals have emerged as a prominent platform for celebrating Commonwealth literature and fostering cultural exchange. These festivals provide a space for authors, readers, and literary enthusiasts to come together and engage in meaningful discussions, readings, and workshops. They serve as a melting pot of ideas where literary luminaries share their insights, experiences, and craft with an eager audience.

One of the most renowned literary festivals is the Jaipur Literature Festival, held annually in India. This festival attracts well-known Commonwealth authors and emerging voices to engage in lively discussions on various themes, ranging from political activism to spirituality. The festival offers a glimpse into the diverse literary landscape of the Commonwealth, promoting cross-cultural understanding and appreciation.

Another notable literary festival is the Edinburgh International Book Festival, which is held in Scotland. This festival brings authors from the Commonwealth and beyond, inviting them to share their works and engage in thought-provoking conversations. From book signings to panel discussions, the festival creates a vibrant atmosphere where literature catalyses dialogue and unity.

These literary festivals celebrate the richness of Commonwealth literature and act as a platform for emerging writers to gain recognition and connect with a global audience. They inspire aspiring authors to explore their unique voices and contribute to the ever-evolving tapestry of Commonwealth literature.

In conclusion, Commonwealth literature and literary festivals play a significant role in fostering unity and diversity. They provide a platform for authors to share their stories, promote cross-cultural understanding, and celebrate the shared heritage of the

Commonwealth nations. By engaging with Commonwealth literature and participating in literary festivals, readers can embark on a journey of exploration and appreciation, discovering the power of words to bridge gaps and build connections across borders.

Commonwealth Music and Performing Arts

As we delve into the rich tapestry of the Commonwealth Chronicles, we cannot ignore the vibrant and diverse world of music and performing arts encapsulating the spirit of unity and diversity within the Commonwealth. From the rhythmic beats of Africa to the enchanting melodies of the Caribbean, this subchapter explores the power of music and the performing arts in bringing people together from all corners of the Commonwealth.

Music is a universal language that transcends boundaries and connects people deeply emotionally. Within the Commonwealth, music has played a pivotal role in expressing cultural identity and promoting unity. From traditional folk music to modern genres, the Commonwealth boasts extensive musical styles and traditions that reflect its diverse heritage.

One cannot discuss Commonwealth music without acknowledging the profound influence of African rhythms and melodies. From the vibrant sounds of Afrobeat in Nigeria to the soul-stirring songs of South African jazz, African music has captivated audiences worldwide. African music has become a symbol of resilience and hope within the Commonwealth through its infectious beats and uplifting messages.

The Caribbean, another cultural hub within the Commonwealth, has also made indelible contributions to the world of music and performing arts. Caribbean music has become synonymous with celebration and joy, from the pulsating rhythms of Reggae in Jamaica to the joyous calypso of Trinidad and Tobago. The vibrant and colourful carnivals across the Caribbean showcase the vitality of the region's performing arts, combining music, dance, and elaborate costumes in a spectacle that unites people of all backgrounds.

Beyond these regional influences, the Commonwealth celebrates various classical and contemporary music genres. From the classical compositions of India to the modern pop sensations emerging from Australia and

Canada, the Commonwealth has nurtured countless musical talents that have left an indelible mark on the global stage.

The performing arts, including dance, theatre, and storytelling, also play a crucial role in the cultural fabric of the Commonwealth. Traditional dance forms, such as the graceful ballet of England or the energetic bhangra of India, showcase the diversity of movement and expression within the Commonwealth. Conventional and avant-garde theatrical performances have allowed artists to explore social issues and challenge societal norms.

In conclusion, the Commonwealth is a treasure trove of music and performing arts that transcend borders and unite people through its rich tapestry of sounds, rhythms, and expressions. The melodies and performances that emanate from the Commonwealth tell stories of unity, diversity, and shared experiences. As we continue our exploration of the Commonwealth Chronicles, let us celebrate the power of music and the performing arts in fostering understanding, appreciation, and harmony among all its peoples.

Commonwealth Cuisine and Food Festivals

Food is a universal language that brings people together; nowhere is this more evident than in the Commonwealth. With their rich cultural diversity and culinary traditions, Commonwealth nations offer tempting flavours and food festivals celebrating their unique heritage. In this subchapter, we will delve into the fascinating world of Commonwealth cuisine and explore some of the most remarkable food festivals that showcase the unity and diversity of the Commonwealth nations.

Commonwealth cuisine is a tapestry of flavours and techniques passed down through generations, from India's aromatic spices to Scotland's hearty stews. This culinary diversity reflects the historical connections and cultural exchanges between the nations of the Commonwealth. Whether it's the comforting taste of fish and chips in England or the fragrant curries of the Caribbean, each dish tells a story and represents a vibrant culinary tradition.

One of the best ways to experience Commonwealth cuisine is through food festivals that bring together the best chefs, local producers, and food enthusiasts. These festivals showcase each nation's unique flavours and cooking styles, offering a feast for the senses. For example, the Commonwealth Food Festival held annually in London brings together the cuisines of all 54 member nations, allowing visitors to sample delicacies from around the world. It is a celebration of the diverse culinary heritage and a testament to the power of food in fostering unity.

Another notable food festival is the Flavors of the Commonwealth, held in Melbourne, Australia. This festival focuses on showcasing the multicultural flavours of the Commonwealth nations, with food stalls offering dishes from India, Malaysia, South Africa, and many others. Visitors can indulge in a gastronomic journey, exploring the diverse cuisines and learning about the cultural significance of each dish.

In addition to these large-scale festivals, many Commonwealth nations hold food celebrations. For instance, the Taste of Barbados Festival highlights the island's vibrant culinary scene, featuring local delicacies such as flying fish and cou-cou paired with rum-based cocktails. These festivals promote tourism and serve as platforms for cultural exchange, fostering understanding and appreciation for the diverse heritage of the Commonwealth.

In conclusion, Commonwealth cuisine and food festivals are a testament to the unity and diversity of the member nations. Through the flavours and aromas of their traditional dishes, the Commonwealth nations showcase their rich cultural heritage. Attending these food festivals offers a unique opportunity to embark on a culinary journey, experiencing the vibrant tastes and traditions that bind the Commonwealth together. So, whether you are a food enthusiast or simply curious about different cultures, these festivals will undoubtedly leave you with a deeper appreciation for the power of food to bring people together.

Chapter 8

The Future of the Commonwealth

Strengthening Unity and Diversity

In the diverse tapestry of the Commonwealth, unity, and diversity stand as two essential pillars that have shaped and enriched its history. The Commonwealth Chronicles: Tales of Unity and Diversity explores the remarkable narratives that exemplify the strength found in the unity of its member nations and the beauty derived from their diversity. This subchapter delves into the significance of strengthening unity while celebrating the uniqueness of each Commonwealth nation.

Unity within the Commonwealth has been an enduring force, binding countries across continents and cultures. It is through shared values, such as democracy, human rights, and the rule of law, that member nations have fostered strong relationships. Despite the vast differences in language, customs, and traditions, the Commonwealth has continuously strived to find common ground, promoting a sense of belonging and camaraderie among its people.

However, the strength of the Commonwealth lies not only in unity but also in the celebration of diversity. With a rich tapestry of cultures, languages, and histories, the Commonwealth represents a remarkable mosaic of human experiences. From the bustling streets of Delhi to the serene landscapes of New Zealand, each nation brings its unique flavours to the table, contributing to a vibrant and dynamic collective. By valuing and preserving this diversity, the Commonwealth ensures that no voice goes unheard and that every culture is respected and cherished.

Fostering mutual understanding and respect among member nations is crucial to strengthening unity and diversity within the Commonwealth. This can be achieved through increased cultural exchanges, educational programs, and collaborative initiatives. By facilitating dialogue and cooperation, the Commonwealth can break down barriers, promote intercultural awareness, and cultivate a sense of global citizenship.

Moreover, the Commonwealth must also address the challenges and disparities within its diverse member nations. The Commonwealth can demonstrate the power of collective action and solidarity by working together to tackle poverty, inequality, and climate change. This shared responsibility reinforces the bonds of unity and ensures no nation is left behind in pursuing progress and prosperity.

The Commonwealth Chronicles: Tales of Unity and Diversity invites readers to explore the extraordinary stories that exemplify the strength found in the unity of the Commonwealth and the beauty derived from its diversity. It encourages individuals from all walks of life to embrace the values of harmony and diversity in their communities, fostering a sense of togetherness and respect for differences. Through collective efforts, the Commonwealth can continue to be a shining example of how unity and diversity coexist harmoniously, creating a brighter future for all.

Expanding Commonwealth Membership

The Commonwealth has always been a unique and diverse organisation, bringing together nations from around the globe. Its rich tapestry of cultures, histories, and traditions has symbolised unity and strength. This subchapter explores the fascinating journey of expanding Commonwealth membership and its significance for member countries and the world.

Throughout its history, the Commonwealth has gradually expanded its membership. From its humble beginnings with just a handful of nations, it has grown to include 54 member countries. Each new addition to the Commonwealth family brings unique perspectives, experiences, and contributions, enriching the collective strength of the organisation.

Expanding Commonwealth membership is not merely about increasing numbers but about fostering unity and promoting shared values. The Commonwealth creates a platform for dialogue, understanding, and collaboration by embracing countries from diverse regions and backgrounds. This inclusivity is a testament to the organisation's commitment to promoting peace, democracy, and human rights worldwide.

New members joining the Commonwealth benefit from a range of advantages. The organisation provides a supportive network for countries to share knowledge, best practices, and resources. Member countries collaborate through various programs and initiatives on sustainable development, trade, education, and healthcare. This collective effort helps to address common challenges and create a better future for all citizens.

Understanding the significance of expanding Commonwealth membership is crucial for the general audience. It showcases the power of diversity and emphasises the importance of global cooperation. This subchapter aims to inspire individuals to appreciate and celebrate cultural differences by highlighting the stories of member countries and their unique contributions.

To the Commonwealth audience, this subchapter serves as a reminder of the organisation's strength and resilience. It demonstrates the continued relevance of the Commonwealth in an ever-changing world. By expanding membership, the

Commonwealth ensures its values and principles are upheld and remains a vital force for positive change.

In conclusion, expanding Commonwealth membership is a testament to the organisation's commitment to unity, diversity, and global cooperation. As the Commonwealth family grows, so does its ability to address common challenges, promote peace, and foster sustainable development. By embracing new member countries, the Commonwealth strengthens its position as a beacon of hope and inspiration for the world.

Addressing Emerging Challenges

In the ever-evolving landscape of the Commonwealth, it is crucial to confront and overcome the emerging challenges that arise. The world is constantly changing, and as a diverse community, we must adapt and find innovative solutions to ensure unity and progress. In this subchapter of "Commonwealth Chronicles: Tales of Unity and Diversity," we delve into some of the critical challenges the Commonwealth faces in the present era and explore potential avenues for addressing them.

One of the significant challenges faced by the Commonwealth is climate change. As a global concern, climate change affects all member nations, albeit to varying degrees. Addressing this challenge requires collective action, where countries collaborate and exchange knowledge to mitigate the effects of climate change. By sharing best practices and investing in sustainable technologies, the Commonwealth can combat this existential threat.

Another emerging challenge lies in the realm of economic disparity. While the Commonwealth encompasses countries at various stages of development, there is a pressing need to bridge the gaps between the rich and the poor. We can ensure that all member nations thrive together by fostering inclusive economic growth and reducing inequality. This can be achieved by promoting entrepreneurship, investing in education and skills development, and enhancing trade and economic cooperation among member states.

In today's digital age, the Commonwealth faces new challenges related to technology and cybersecurity. As more member nations embrace digitalisation, addressing data protection, online privacy, and cyber threats becomes imperative. Building robust cybersecurity frameworks, promoting digital literacy, and fostering international collaboration can help safeguard the Commonwealth's digital infrastructure and ensure the secure use of technology for the benefit of all.

Furthermore, amidst the diverse cultures and traditions within the Commonwealth, social cohesion remains a challenge. It is vital to promote understanding, tolerance, and respect among member nations to embrace the shared values of unity and diversity. Encouraging cultural exchanges, fostering dialogue, and celebrating common heritage can foster a sense of belonging and strengthen the bonds within the Commonwealth.

In conclusion, the Commonwealth must proactively address the emerging challenges it faces to foster unity and diversity. By tackling climate change, economic disparity, technology, and social cohesion, member nations can work together to create a brighter, more sustainable future. Through collaboration, cooperation, and collective action, the Commonwealth can overcome these challenges and continue to thrive as a global community.

Chapter 9

Conclusion: Celebrating Unity in Diversity through the Commonwealth

In this final chapter of "Commonwealth Chronicles: Tales of Unity and Diversity," we reflect upon the extraordinary journey we have taken together, celebrating the essence of unity within the vast diversity of the Commonwealth. Throughout this book, we have explored the stories, cultures, and shared values that bind the member nations of the Commonwealth, highlighting the strength of our collective voice. As we conclude our exploration, we are inspired by the potential for a brighter future built upon the foundation of unity and diversity.

The Commonwealth, with its 54 member nations spanning across six continents, is a true testament to the power of unity in diversity. Despite our language, religion, and customs differences, we have embraced the idea that our shared history, values, and aspirations can bridge any divide. Through the Commonwealth, we have fostered meaningful connections, deepened understanding, and harnessed our collective strength to address global challenges.

One of the most remarkable aspects of the Commonwealth is the respect and appreciation for diversity ingrained in its fabric. Our member nations are a tapestry of cultures, traditions, and experiences, and through this diversity, we find our greatest strength. We have fostered innovation, creativity, and progress by embracing our differences and promoting inclusive societies. The Commonwealth stands as a shining example of how diversity can be a driving force for positive change.

This book delves into the stories of individuals and communities who have exemplified unity in diversity. From the indigenous peoples of Australia to the vibrant cultures of Africa and the Caribbean, we have witnessed the rich tapestry of our shared heritage. We have explored the challenges member nations face and the resilience that has allowed us to overcome adversity together. These tales of unity and diversity have showcased the beauty and potential within the Commonwealth.

As we celebrate the conclusion of this journey, we are reminded of the importance of nurturing and cherishing the Commonwealth's values. These values of democracy, human rights, and sustainable development provide the guiding principles that will shape our shared future. By upholding these ideals, we can continue building bridges, fostering understanding, and creating a more equitable and inclusive world.

In conclusion, "Commonwealth Chronicles: Tales of Unity and Diversity" has offered a glimpse into the remarkable tapestry of cultures, histories, and aspirations that define the Commonwealth. By celebrating unity in diversity, we have laid the foundation for a future where collaboration, understanding, and respect prevail. Let us continue to cherish the Commonwealth's spirit of inclusivity and strive towards a world where unity thrives and diversity is celebrated.